Telling Time with the Judy Clock

Written by Cindy Barden

Illustrated by Becky J. Radtke

 Judy/Instructo, Torrance, California

 **Judy/Instructo**®

Executive Editor: Douglas M. Rife
Editor: Lisa Schwimmer Marier

 Design and Production
by Good Neighbor Press, Inc., Grand Junction, CO.

Published by Judy/Instructo, Parsippany, NJ 07054

ISBN 1-56417-839-0

Printed in the United States of America
1.987654

Table of Contents

Oh, That Face!

Lights! Camera! Action! The lights go up and center stage is Arnold Schwarzenegger, the muscled behemoth star of action movies, sitting on the set of a typical kindergarten classroom. Look closely and, amid the clutter, you will see the Judy Clock sharing center stage in the movie "Kindergarten Cop." This is a classic case of art imitating life. Kindergarten, first-, and second-grade classrooms all across America and Canada display and use the Judy Clock. Not as a prop but as a valuable teaching tool.

The Judy Clock hasn't always freelanced as a movie star. The clock got its start as a classroom aid to help teachers teach telling time. The official patent for the Judy Clock was granted to Mr. Hyman Berman on March 25, 1952. Mr. Berman was the founder of the Judy Company. In 1937, Mrs. Ruth Berman, his wife, went into downtown Minneapolis to buy a birthday present for their daughter, Judy. She brought home a fifty-cent toy for Judy. When Mr. Berman, then a chemist, saw the toy, he noted that he could make a better one in his home workshop. Mr. Berman created a small woodboard puzzle. That puzzle was the beginning of the Judy Company named, of course, for his daughter. The puzzle was so admired, that many of his friends suggested Mr. Berman make puzzles for sale to the general public. His hobby turned into a thriving business. The puzzle line expanded and, in 1952, he introduced the Judy Clock as one of the company's products.

In 1986, The Judy/Instructo Company and its *star*, the Judy Clock, joined the Simon & Schuster family of companies. That Judy Clock face, recognized by teachers, parents, and children, has been starring in classrooms all across the continent for well over forty years! Now, that is star quality!

Telling Time

Using the Judy Clock

The *Telling Time with the Judy Clock* book was developed to provide teachers with reproducibles to use while teaching the concept of time with the Judy Clock. These activities are organized in the book from the most simple activities to the more difficult. The activities are meant to be used for written practice while children are learning to tell time.

The reproducibles begin with the most basic concepts and progress to the more complicated, enabling you to work through the unit successively. These reproducibles can also be used to reinforce concepts children are having difficulty with as well as for review.

Below are some suggestions for introducing the concepts for telling time as well as teaching options to use throughout the unit. You may pick and choose those options that are most appropriate for your children.

Hands-On Activities

As students practice telling time through the step-by-step activities in this book, you can demonstrate each step with the Judy Clock. "Mini- clocks" from the *Telling Time with the Judy Clock* book are an inexpensive way to provide hands-on experience for every child.

Different hands-on experiences can help children understand the concept of measuring time. Have children make their own clocks from paper plates, attaching paper hands with a metal brad. Or, you may choose to use devices like an egg timer, stopwatch, or even a sundial to help students "see" time passing.

You can find several simple hands-on projects in *Clocks: Building and Experimenting with Model Timepieces* by Bernie Zubrowski (Boston Children's Museum, Morrow Junior Books, 1988). Other books about time are included in the bibliography at the end of the book.

Estimate Time

Give the children opportunities to practice estimating how long various activities will take. Give students a list of activities, such as climbing a ladder, walking a specific distance, reading a story, saying the alphabet, or counting to 100. Ask them to estimate how long they think each activity will take. Encourage children to compare their estimates with those made by other classmates. The children can then do the specific activity and compare their estimates to the actual time elapsed.

Compare and Contrast

As you study time-measuring devices, have children explore and compare other types of measuring devices, such as rulers, teaspoons, pints, and quarts. Encourage them to look for similarities by comparing a clock to a ruler, a measuring cup to a stopwatch, or a calendar to a timeline.

Use "What if?" for Group Discussions

Asking "What if?" questions provides children with opportunities for critical thinking. Here are some "What if's" you can use.

- What if both hands of a clock were the same size?
- What if all the clocks in the world stopped at the same time?
- How did people tell time before they had clocks?
- What if you traveled from California to New York in one day? Would the time be different in New York?
- What if you could save good times and live them over again?
- What if you could travel to any time in the world? Where and when would you go? Why?

Encourage children to think up and discuss their own "What if" questions. You'll find other topics to use for group discussions throughout the book.

Schedules

Use a local bus or subway schedule or a copy of a TV program listing to help children understand schedules, what they are used for, and why they are helpful. Ask children to make up their own schedules for events for a specific day or week.

Hold Timed Events

To help children understand elapsed time, hold timed events. Have children be the timekeepers. Some activities could be: a jelly-bean eating contest; seeing who can do the most push-ups, sit-ups, or jumping jacks in one minute; and timing events like blowing up a balloon, tying 10 shoes, playing a game of checkers, or carrying a peanut across the gym on a spoon without dropping it.

Telling Time with the Judy Clock

The activities and reproducibles in this teacher's resource are designed to go from simple to more complex, in the order they are presented here. You may choose, however, to set up your own schedule of activities, changing the order to what is most appropriate for your children.

Name _____

Parts of the Clock

Judy Clock

hours · minute hand · hour hand · clock face · each scallop shows one minute · minutes after the hour

Name _____

Morning and Night

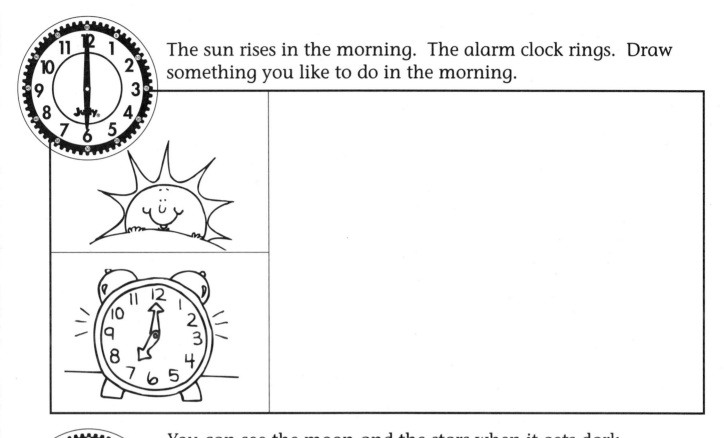

The sun rises in the morning. The alarm clock rings. Draw something you like to do in the morning.

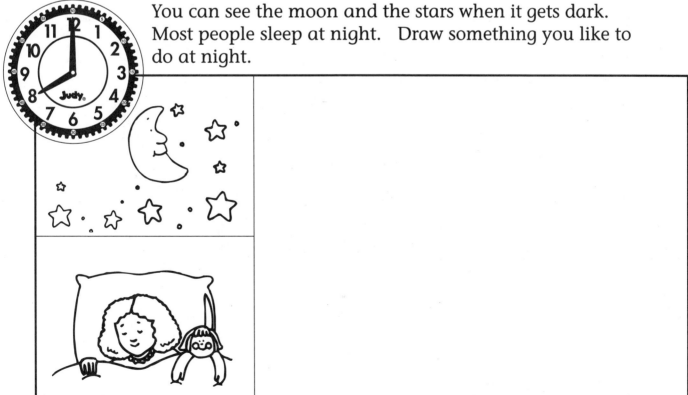

You can see the moon and the stars when it gets dark. Most people sleep at night.   Draw something you like to do at night.

Name _____

Morning or Night?

Circle the pictures that show things you do in the morning. Draw a square around pictures that show things you do at night.

Discussion Topic
What is your favorite time of day? Why?

                                                                                 J209039

Less Time

Do both activities shown in each box. Circle the one that takes less time.

tying your shoe

writing your name

hopping 10 times

playing checkers

drawing an elephant

making a paper fan

solving a puzzle alone

solving a puzzle with friends

Name _____

More Time

Circle the activity in each box you think takes more time.

                                                    J209039

Name _____

More Time or Less Time?

Draw pictures of two things that take **more** time than tying your shoe.

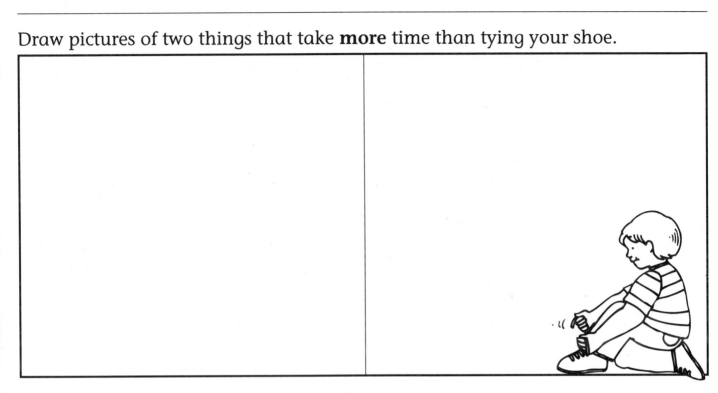

Draw pictures of two things that take **less** time than building a sand castle.

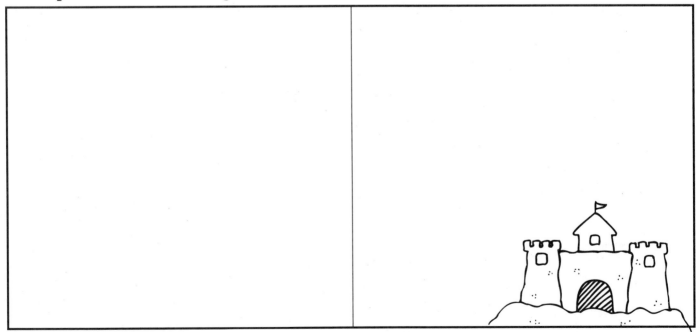

How many clocks can you find around your house? Don't forget to count watches, clocks on stoves, computers, and clock radios. If you have a basement or a garage, check there for clocks, too!

Write the Numbers

Follow the dotted lines to write the numbers on the clock.

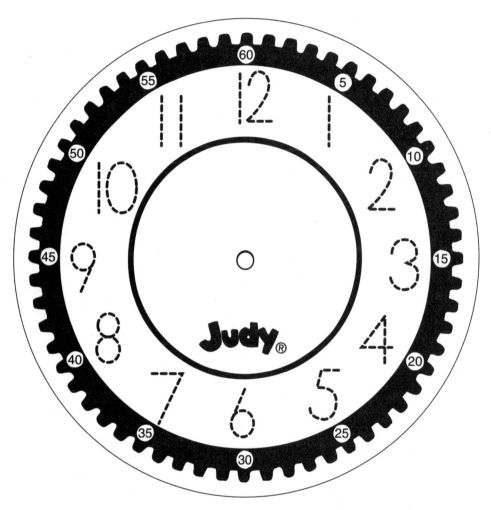

The Egyptians were probably the first to divide days into 24 hours—about 6,000 years ago.

Write in the missing numbers.

1 2 ___ 4 5 ___ 7 8 ___ 10 ___ 12

1 ___ 3 ___ 5 ___ 7 ___ 9 ___ 11 ___

                                          J209039

The Clock

Write the missing numbers on the clocks.

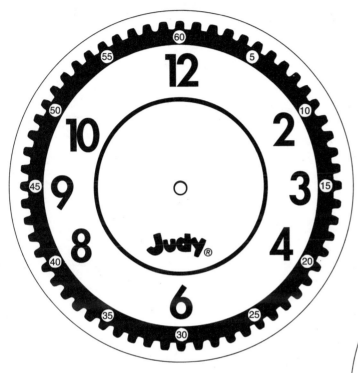

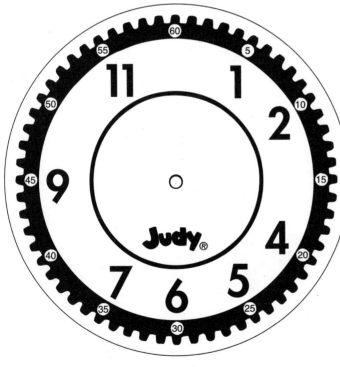

Discussion Topics
1. Why do we need clocks?
2. What if we didn't have any clocks?

The Minute Hand and the Hour Hand

The short hand on the clock is called the **hour hand.** It is the s-l-o-w hand.

The long hand on the clock is called the **minute hand.** It moves faster than the hour hand.

Color the **hour hand** red. Color the **minute hand** blue.

A clock in Toi, Japan, has a face 101 feet in diameter. The large hand is 41 feet long!

J209039

Draw the Hands on the Clock

Circle the **minute hand**.

Circle the **hour hand**.

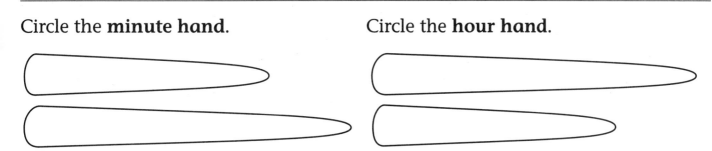

Draw a **minute hand** on the clock. Make it point to the 12.

Draw an **hour hand** on the clock. Make it point to the 4.

The hands on
the clock
always move
this way.

Discussion Topics
1. What if clocks didn't have hands?
2. Why do you think the pointers on a clock are called hands?

Where Do the Hands Point?

Where do the hands point? Write the numbers on the line.

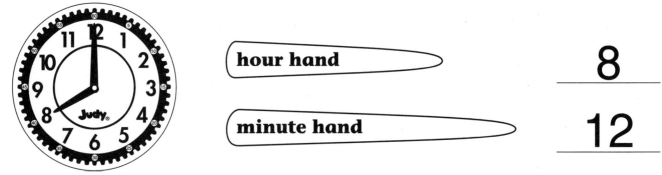

hour hand __8__

minute hand __12__

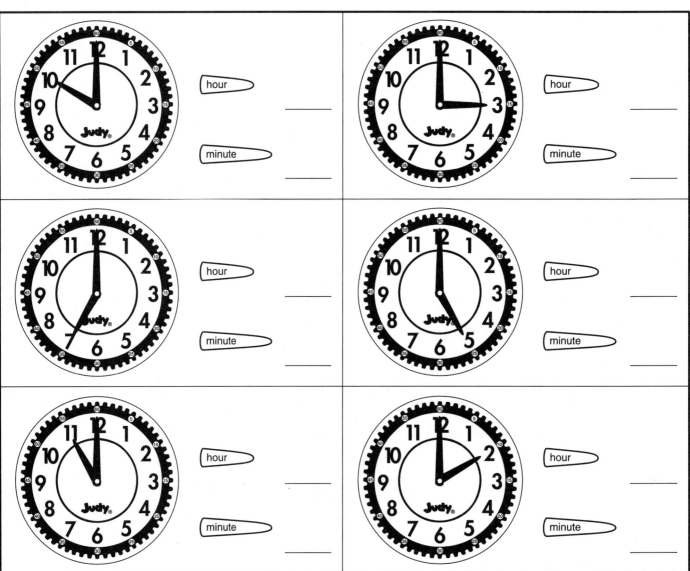

hour _____

minute _____

hour _____

minute _____

hour _____

minute _____

hour _____

minute _____

hour _____

minute _____

hour _____

minute _____

What is the same about the **minute hand** on every one of these clocks?

J209039

Name _____

What's the "O'Clock"?

The **hour hand** points to the number that tells us the "o'clock."

When the **hour hand** points to 4 and the **minute hand** points to 12, it is 4 o'clock.

_____4_____ o'clock

Pretend your arms are the hands of the clock. Show where your arms would point at 3:00, at 9:00, and at 4:00. Where would your arms be at 12:00?

Where does the **hour hand** point? Write the number in the blank below each clock.

_____ o'clock   _____ o'clock   _____ o'clock

_____ o'clock   _____ o'clock   _____ o'clock

Another Way to Write It

4:00 is another way to write 4 o'clock.

4 o'clock
4:00

Write the time two
ways beside each clock.

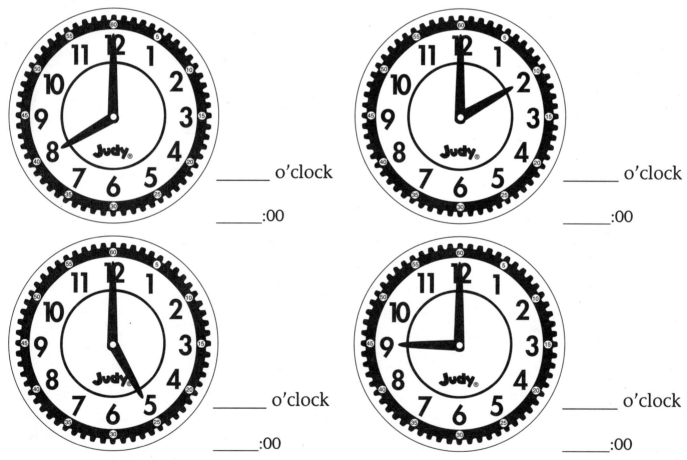

_____ o'clock

_____ :00

_____ o'clock

_____ :00

_____ o'clock

_____ :00

_____ o'clock

_____ :00

Discussion Topic
When it's 4 o'clock, we write 4:00. The 4 tells the hour. What do you think the
00 at the end means?

                                                                              J209039

Draw the Hour Hand

Draw the **hour hand** on each clock to show the time.

 **8 o'clock**

7 o'clock

4 o'clock

11 o'clock

9:00

2:00

7:00

Name _____

Draw Both Hands on the Clocks

Draw the **hour hand** and the **minute hand** on each clock to show the time.

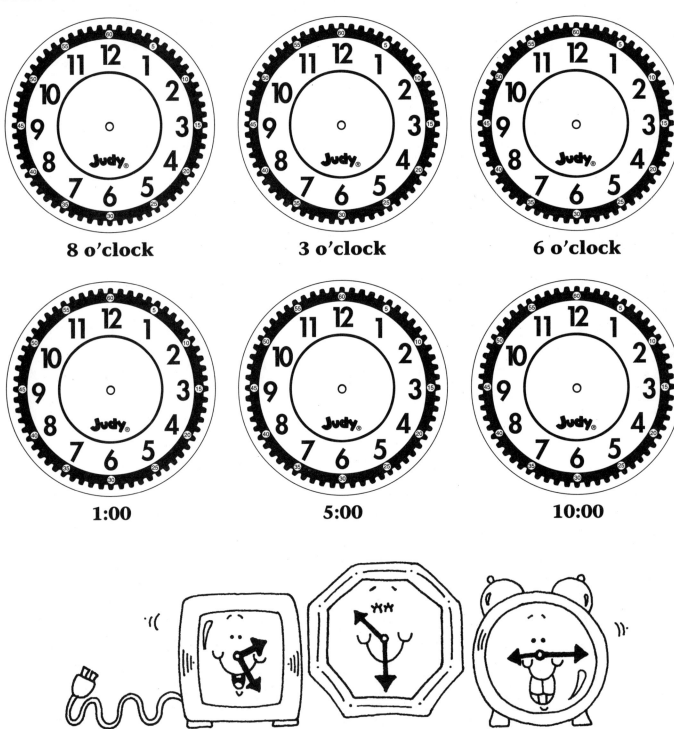

8 o'clock   **3 o'clock**   **6 o'clock**

1:00   **5:00**   **10:00**

Discussion Topic
Does the shape of the clock change how we tell time?

J209039

Name _____

Digital Clocks

Some clocks have no hands. They are called **digital clocks.**

Both clocks show the
same time.
It is 7 o'clock.

Draw a line to connect the clocks that show the same time.

Discussion Topic

Clocks that have hands are called **analog** clocks. Clocks that do not have hands
are called **digital** clocks. Which kind of clock do you like best? Why?

What Do You Do?

Draw a picture to show something you do at the times on each clock.

Cut out pictures of clocks and watches from magazines and catalogs. Work with a group to make a "Time" collage.

Name _____

How Long Is a Minute?

Line up and begin walking when your teacher says start. Your teacher will say stop when one minute is up. How far did you walk?

How many times do you think you can write your name in one minute? Try it while your teacher times you.

_____

- -

_____

- -

_____

- -

_____

- - - - - - - - - - - - - - - - - - - -

_____

- - - - - - - - - - - - - - - - - - - -

_____

- - - - - - - - - - - - - - - - - - - -

_____

It takes about one minute to blow a really big bubble.
How long do you think it would take to clean the gum off your face if the bubble bursts?

You can sing the main verse of Jingle Bells 7 times in one minute. Try it.

Jingle bells, jingle bells,
Jingle all the way.
Oh, what fun it is to ride
In a one-horse open sleigh.
Hey!

Discussion Topics
What do you think this saying means? *Time flies when you're having fun.*

Name _____

More or Less than a Minute?

Does it take more or less than a minute? Circle *more* or *less*.

Bake a cake.
more   less

Climb a ladder.
more   less

Do three jumping jacks.
more   less

Walk to school.
more   less

Eat supper.
more   less

Sneeze
more   less

Draw something you could do in about 1 minute.

Dan Jansen set a new world speed-skating record for the 1,000 meter race at the 1994 Olympics. He finished the race in 1 minute, 12.43 seconds.

J209039

Name _____

Minutes and Hours

An hour is much longer than a minute.

How long will it take? Circle *minutes* or *hours*.

60 minutes = 1 hour.

Get dressed like a clown.

minutes   hours

Eat an ice-cream cone.

minutes   hours

Paint a long fence.

minutes   hours

Make your bed.

minutes   hours

Draw something you could do in about 1 hour.

Half Hours

Where do the hands point? Write the numbers on the line.

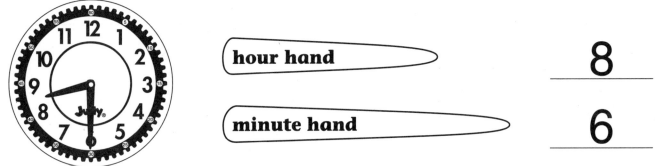

hour hand   8

minute hand   6

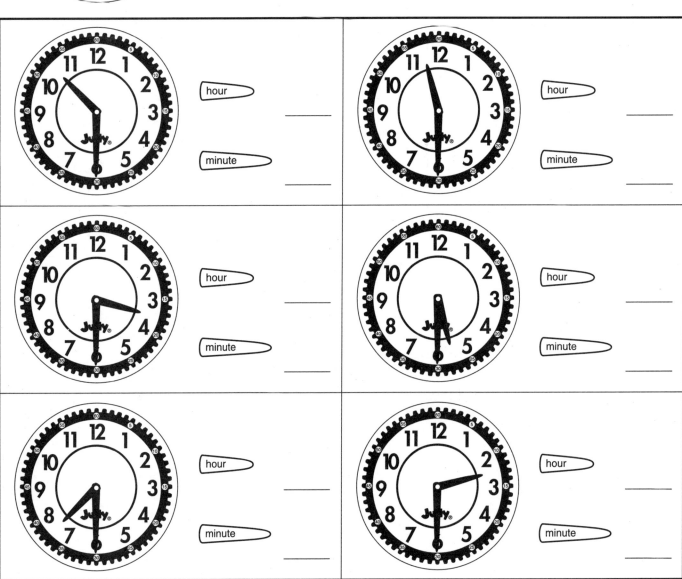

hour   _____

minute   _____

hour   _____

minute   _____

hour   _____

minute   _____

hour   _____

minute   _____

hour   _____

minute   _____

hour   _____

minute   _____

What is the same about the **minute hand** on every one of these clocks?

Reading the Half Hours

9:30

On a clock, the 12 is at the top. The 6 is at the bottom. Point to the 12 and the 6 on the clock below.

When the **minute hand** points to the 6, it is halfway around the clock.

½ hour = 30 minutes

Look closely at the clock. The **hour hand** is not exactly on the 9. It is about halfway between the 9 and 10.

Draw the **minute hand** to show the time on the clocks below.

1:30	12:30	10:30
4:30	**3:30**	**8:30**

Name _____

Different Ways to Write 4:30

There are four ways to write 4:30. They all mean the same.

4:30
Four-thirty
Half past 4
30 minutes
  after 4

Look at the **hour hand**.
Why do you think it is
between numbers?

Write the numbers and number words under the clocks.

_____:30   _____:30   _____:30

_____-thirty   _____-thirty   _____-thirty

30 minutes after _____   30 minutes after _____   30 minutes after _____

Half past _____   Half past _____   Half past _____

Review Number Words

1 one	2 two	3 three	4 four	5 five	6 six
7 seven	8 eight	9 nine	10 ten	11 eleven	12 twelve

© 1995 Judy/Instructo
J209039

Draw the Hands for the Half Hours

Draw the **minute hand** and the **hour hand** on each clock to show the time.

30 minutes after 7

30 minutes before 12

Eleven-thirty

8:30

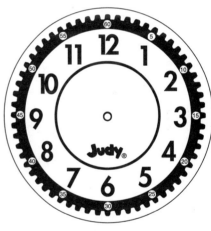

30 minutes after 5

Half past 2

Five-thirty

9:30

Quarter Hours

When the **minute hand** points to the 3, it is 15 minutes after the hour.

There are three ways to write 7:15. They all mean the same.

| 15 minutes after = quarter after |

7:15
15 minutes after 7
Quarter after 7

Draw the **minute hand** to show the time.

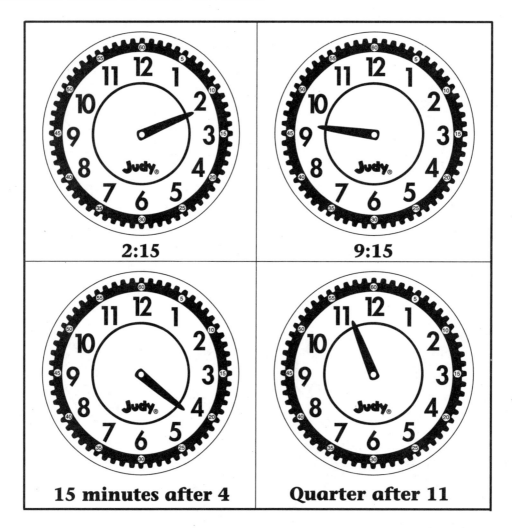

2:15

9:15

15 minutes after 4

Quarter after 11

J209039

Match the Hours, Halves, and Quarters

Draw a line to connect the clocks to the correct time.

   **one-thirty**

   **2:15**

                                   9 o'clock

                                   quarter past 3

                                   quarter after 11

                                   10:30

   **15 minutes after 7**

                                   8:00

Name _____

Counting By Fives

To tell time, it helps if you can count by fives. Practice counting by fives a few times.

5 10 15 20 25 30 35 40 45 50 55 60

Close your eyes and try it again. Did you get it right? If not, keep practicing.

Look at the clock. Point to each number, starting at 1. Count by fives. When you get to the 12, you should be at 60. It takes 5 minutes for the **minute hand** to get to each number on the clock.

What number is in the circle by the 3? _____

What number is in the circle by the 6? _____

What number is in the circle by the 8? _____

What number is in the circle by the 11? _____

Discussion Topic:
Why do you think the numbers are in the circle? What do you think they mean?

J209039

Counting Minutes

Fill in the missing numbers in the circles on the clock. Remember to count by fives.

Judy®

Fill in the missing numbers.

5 ____ 15 ____ 25 ____ 35 ____ 45 ____ 55 ____

The three-toed sloth of South America travels at a speedy 6 to 8 feet per minute on the ground. At that rate, it would take a sloth between 11 and 14 hours to travel one mile!

Three-Quarters of an Hour

When the **minute hand** points to the 9, it is three-quarters after the hour. Count by fives. You will see it is the same as 45 minutes after 4. Try it.

There are four ways to write the time. They all mean exactly the same thing.

4:45
45 minutes after 4
15 minutes before 5
Quarter to 5

Three-quarters of an hour = 45 minutes.

Now try this: Start at the 9 and count by fives. Stop when you get to the 12.

5	—	10	—	15
(9 to 10)		(10 to 11)		(11 to 12)

When the **minute hand** is on the 9, it is 15 minutes before the next hour. Look at the **hour hand**. It is almost to the 5.

You could watch a one hour TV program in three-quarters of an hour—if there weren't any commercials.

You could clean your room in 45 minutes—if it's not too messy.

J209039

How about the One and Two?

You know how to read a clock when the **minute hand** points to the 12, the 3, the 6, and the 9. Learning the rest of the numbers is easy!

When the **minute hand** is on the 1, it is 5 minutes after the hour.

4:05 means the same as 5 minutes after 4.

When the **minute hand** is on the 2, it is 10 minutes after the hour.

4:10 means the same as 10 minutes after 4.

Write the time below the clocks.

_____   _____   _____   _____

Draw both hands on these clocks to show the correct time:

10 minutes after 1

5 minutes after 10

10 minutes after 12

5 minutes after 2

Name _____

Now You're Ready for the Four and Five

Count by fives to the 4 and the 5. Start at the 12.

5 — 10 — 15 — 20 — 25

When the **minute hand** is on the 4, it is 20 minutes after the hour.

4:20 means the same as 20 minutes after 4.

When the **minute hand** is on the 5, it is 25 minutes after the hour.

4:25 means the same as 25 minutes after 4.

Draw both hands on the clocks below to show the correct time.

20 after 10   **25 after 11**   **25 after 4**   **20 after 8**

Write the time below each clock.

_____   _____   _____   _____

Seven and Eight, It's Getting Late

When the **minute hand** has passed the 6, it is on its way to the next "o'clock."
Look at the **hour hand**. It's getting closer to the 5.

4:35
35 minutes after 4
25 minutes to 5
25 to 5

When the **minute hand** is on the 7, it is 35 minutes **after** the hour. It is also 25 minutes **before** the next hour.

4:40
40 minutes after 4
20 minutes to 5
20 to 5

When the **minute hand** is on the 8, it is 40 minutes **after** the hour. It is also 20 minutes **before** the next hour.

Write the time below each clock.

_____ _____ _____ _____

Draw the hands on the clocks to show the correct time.

35 minutes after 2 **20 to 9** **25 minutes to 5** **40 minutes after 7**

Ten and Eleven-That's All, Folks!

The **hour hand** has moved almost to the 5. It's almost 5 o'clock.

4:50
50 minutes after 4
10 minutes to 5
10 to 5

When the **minute hand** is on the 10, it is 50 minutes **after** the hour. It is also 10 minutes **before** the next hour.

4:55
55 minutes after 4
5 minutes to 5
5 to 5

When the **minute hand** is on the 11, it is 55 minutes **after** the hour. It is also 5 minutes **before** the next hour.

Write the time below each clock.

_____ _____ _____ _____

Draw the hands on the clocks to show the correct time.

10 to 1   **5 minutes to 4**   **50 minutes after 7**   **55 minutes after 12**

© 1995 Judy/Instructo
J209039

The Marks Between the Numbers

Just when you thought you had learned everything you needed to tell time, here comes something else. But don't worry. This is the easy part.

Look at the clock. See the marks between the numbers? There are four marks between each number. The mark on the number makes five.

Each mark equals one minute.

To find the exact time, look at the **minute hand**. Count by fives to the last number before the **minute hand**. Then add one more minute for each mark.

This clock is set at 4:12. You know that it takes 10 minutes for the **minute hand** to point to the 2. The **minute hand** is pointing to the second mark after the 2.

10 minutes + 2 minutes = 12 minutes

Write the times below each of these clocks.

10:____   7:____   5:____   3:____

How Long Is a Second?

Explain to the students that a second is the smallest unit of time measured by most clocks.

60 seconds = 1 minute

Explain that when clocks have 3 hands, the longest hand is called the second hand. It takes one minute for the second hand to go all the way around. The second hand moves fast.

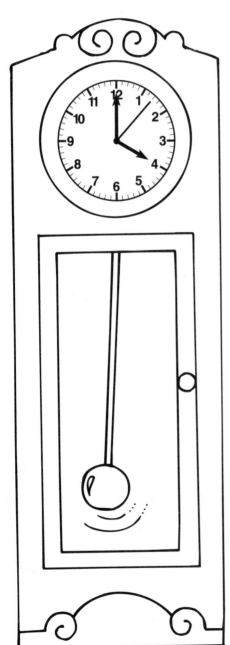

Explain to the class that a minute is made up of 60 seconds and that every second lasts the same amount of time. For instance, it takes about one second to sneeze, turn on a light switch, wiggle your toes or your nose, or say, "More pizza, please."

Encourage children to look at a clock with a second hand. When the second hands gets to the 12, count each second with the children as they watch the second hand move around the clock. Try this activity again, but have them close their eyes and count slowly to 60. Then have them open their eyes and look at the second hand.

Explain that if the second hand is before the 12, they counted too fast. If the second hand is after the 12, they counted too slowly.

Have them try it a few more times to see how closely they can get to counting exactly 60 seconds—1 minute.

The longest Major League baseball game took 8 hours and 6 minutes to play. The Chicago White Sox beat the Milwaukee Brewers 7 to 6 in the 25th inning.

Clinton R. Bailey tied all six Boy Scout Handbook knots (square knot, sheet bend, sheepshank, clove hitch, round turn and two half hitches, and bowline) in a record breaking 8.1 seconds in 1977. It probably took you more than 8.1 second just to read about it!

Name _____

Just a Second

Light travels 186,282 miles per second. Sound travels slower than light. That is why we see lightning before we hear thunder.

It takes about 10 seconds to say the poem, "Hickory, Dickory, Dock." Time it.

A really good yawn takes about 15 seconds. Try it.

Hickory, dickory, dock.
The mouse ran up the clock.
The clock struck one,
And down he run.
Hickory, dickory, dock.

What is something you can do in 1 second?
Draw or write your answer here:

Bobby Unser's pit crew needed only 4 seconds to add fuel to his race car on lap 10 of the Indianapolis 500 in 1976.

In 1978, Wendy Wall set a record for making a bed with two sheets, a blanket, and a pillowcase. She did it in 28.2 seconds.

How Long Did It Take?

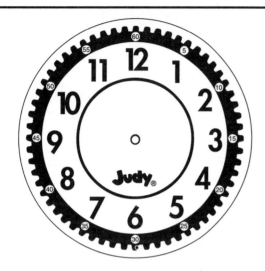

Max stayed at the pool for two hours. He left at 4:20. Draw the hands to show what time he got to the pool.

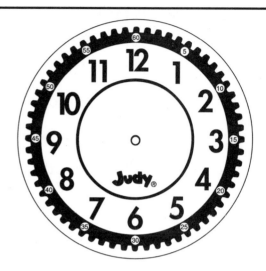

The Eden Angels started playing baseball at 4:00. They were rained out 20 minutes later. Draw the hands on the clock to show what time they were rained out.

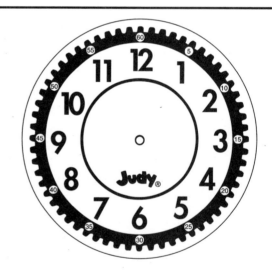

Tanya arrived at the bus stop at 11:15. The bus came 10 minutes later. Draw the hands to show what time the bus arrived.

Time Yourself

How long does it take to walk from your house to a friend's house?

Time Passes

Look at the clock. Tell what time it will be:

In 2 hours: _____

In 20 minutes: _____

In 2 minutes: _____

In 30 minutes: _____

Look at the two clocks. How much time has gone by?

_15_ minutes

_____ minutes

_____ minutes

_____ minutes

If you sleep an average of 8 hours a day, you will spend a total of 2,920 hours a year sleeping. By the time you are 10 years old, you will have slept away more than three years of your life!

Counting Time

Fill in the charts below.

Add 20 minutes

6:00	__6__ : __2__ __0__
8:30	___ : ___ ___
2:25	___ : ___ ___

Add 6 minutes

4:11	___ : ___ ___
6:14	___ : ___ ___
3:54	___ : ___ ___

Add 3 hours

11:19	___ : ___ ___
5:36	___ : ___ ___
7:01	___ : ___ ___

Subtract 2 hours

10:22	___ : ___ ___
9:07	___ : ___ ___
1:15	___ : ___ ___

Subtract 5 minutes

11:55	___ : ___ ___
12:05	___ : ___ ___
10:14	___ : ___ ___

Time Language

First you learned to "read" a clock. Now it's time to learn to "write" in time language.

To write in time language, remember that the hour comes first.

After the hour is a colon. A colon looks like this :

A colon divides the hours and the minutes.

The number of minutes after the hour are written after the colon.

1:10 = Ten minutes after one   **3:26 = Twenty-six minutes after three**

If the number of minutes is nine or less, use a zero before the number: 01, 02, 03, 04, 05, 06, 07, 08, 09

9:07 = Seven minutes after nine.

If it is exactly the "o'clock," write two zeros after the colon. The two zeros mean no minutes after the hour.

12:00 = Twelve o'clock   **5:00 = Five o'clock**

Fill in the blanks with the correct numbers.

   4:58 means _____ minutes after _____ .   1:01 means _____ minute after _____ .

   5:36 means _____ minutes after _____ .   9:29 means _____ minutes after _____ .

Write the time in time language below each clock:

_____ : _____   _____ : _____   _____ : _____

_____ : _____   _____ : _____   _____ : _____

J209039

Name _____

Reading and Writing Time Language

Write these times in time language. Don't forget the colon.

Seven-thirty   _____

Fifteen minutes after six   _____

Quarter to one   _____

Twenty after three   _____

Twenty-five to eight   _____

Eight o'clock   _____

Cross out the time words below each clock that are not correct.

4:30
Four-thirty
20 to 5
30 minutes after 4

Ten to 5
5:50
50 minutes after 5
10 minutes to six

55 minutes after 8
Five to nine
Five after nine
5 to 9

25 after 1
1:25
12:25
35 to 2

35 minutes after 11
11:35
25 minutes to 12
11:25

Twenty to 3
Three twenty
40 minutes after 2
2:40

48

Name _____

Before Noon or After Noon?

Clocks with hands do not tell us if it is morning or afternoon. If the clock says 8:00, how do you know if it's time to eat breakfast or time to go to bed?

That's not too tough. If you just got up, it's time to eat breakfast. Everybody knows that.

What if someone says, I'll call you at 7:15? Will it be in the morning or in the evening?

The initials a.m. are short for the Latin words *ante meridian*. It means "before noon." The time from midnight until noon is followed by a.m. If it's easier to remember, a.m. can also stand for "after midnight."

To show it is before noon, use a.m. after the time numbers.

6:30 a.m. = Thirty minutes after six in the morning.

The initials p.m. are short for the Latin words *post meridian*, meaning "after noon." To show it is after noon, use p.m. after the time numbers.

6:30 p.m. = Thirty minutes after six in the evening.

Add a.m. or p.m. after the times.

Most people eat breakfast around 8:00 _____.

The evening news starts at 6:00 _____.

Morning cartoons start at 5:30 _____.

School starts at 8:30 _____.

School is over at 3:30 _____.

The sun probably isn't shining at 11:14 _____.

Night security guards shouldn't be sleeping at 1:25 _____.

Many young children take an afternoon nap about 2:00 _____.

How would you write these times?

Ten o'clock in the morning. _____

Fifteen minutes after 1 in the afternoon. _____

Thirty minutes past six in the evening. _____

Twenty minutes to nine in the morning. _____

Name _____

One Day at a Time

The Earth spins, like a top. One day equals the time it takes for the Earth to rotate (spin) one time. Each day begins at midnight and lasts for 24 hours.

86,400 seconds = 1 day
1,440 minutes = 1 day
24 hours = 1 day
7 days = 1 week

As the Earth turns, a different part of the Earth faces toward the sun. The part facing the sun has daylight. As it turns away from the sun, it gets darker.

Hold a flashlight about a foot away from a globe. Shine it on the globe while someone slowly turns the globe.

Can you see how different places on Earth have day and night at different times?

Long ago, people made clocks called *sundials*. On sunny days, they could tell time by looking at the shadow. This worked fine on sunny days. What do you think happened on cloudy days and at night?

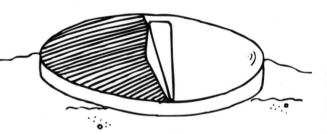

- *In 1991, Ashrita Furman of Jamaica, N.Y., completed 307 hopscotch games in 24 hours.*
- *A baby opossum is born in 8 to 12 days.*
- *It takes 75 to 82 days for the eggs of the wandering albatross to hatch.*
- *Great spotted woodpecker eggs hatch in 10 days.*
- *It would take about 23 days to count to one million if you didn't stop to eat or sleep.*
- *Some types of bamboo can grow up to three feet per day. I'll bet your mother is glad you don't grow that fast!*
- *At Walt Disney World in Orlando, Florida, you'll find the world's largest sundial. It measures 122 feet across the base and is 120 feet high.*

J209039

Some Things Take a Week

604,800 seconds = 1 week
10,080 minutes = 1 week
168 hours = 1 week
7 days = 1 week
52 weeks = 1 year

Many things can happen in a week:

- A tadpole can change into a frog in a week.
- You could catch a cold and get better in a week.
- Your family could spend a week camping at Yellowstone National Park.

If you could plan a one-week family vacation, what would you like to do most? Write your ideas for each day. Show your vacation ideas to your parents. Maybe they would consider some of your ideas for your next vacation.

On Monday,
I would like to _____

On Tuesday,
it would be fun to _____

On Wednesday,
we could _____

On Thursday,
it would be fun to _____

Friday would
be a good day to _____

On Saturday,
I would like to _____

Sunday would
be the best day to _____

Name _____

Learn about a Month

The names of the months are:

JANUARY   FEBRUARY   MARCH   APRIL   MAY   JUNE
JULY   AUGUST   SEPTEMBER   OCTOBER   NOVEMBER   DECEMBER

12 months = 1 year

What month is it right now? _____

What is the name of next month? _____

Which month is your favorite? Make up a story or poem, or draw a picture, to show why you like that month.

Some months have 30 days. Some have 31. February has 28 days, except in leap year. Then it has 29. Here's a poem to remember how many days are in each month:

Thirty days hath September,
April, June, and November.
February has 28 alone,
All the rest have 31,
Excepting leap year; that's the time
When February's days are 29.

- *Duck eggs hatch in about 30 days.*
- *It takes about 31 days for a baby field mouse to be born.*
- *Most people get a haircut about once a month.*
- *It takes about a month for bean seeds to grow into plants—if you remember to water them every few days.*
- *It takes more than 20 months for a baby Asian elephant to be born.*

J209039

1 2 Months Make One Year

Write the number of days in each month in the blanks. Look at the calendar to help you.

JANUARY

M	T	W	TH	F	S	S
1	2	3	4	5	6	7
8	9	10	11	12	13	14
15	16	17	18	19	20	21
22	23	24	25	26	27	28
29	30	31				

January has _____ days

FEBRUARY

M	T	W	TH	F	S	S
			1	2	3	4
5	6	7	8	9	10	11
12	13	14	15	16	17	18
19	20	21	22	23	24	25
26	27	28				

February has _____ days
(29 in leap year)

MARCH

M	T	W	TH	F	S	S
			1	2	3	4
5	6	7	8	9	10	11
12	13	14	15	16	17	18
19	20	21	22	23	24	25
26	27	28	29	30	31	

March has _____ days

APRIL

M	T	W	TH	F	S	S
						1
2	3	4	5	6	7	8
9	10	11	12	13	14	15
16	17	18	19	20	21	22
23	24	25	26	27	28	29
30						

April has _____ days

MAY

M	T	W	TH	F	S	S
	1	2	3	4	5	6
7	8	9	10	11	12	13
14	15	16	17	18	19	20
21	22	23	24	25	26	27
28	29	30	31			

May has _____ days

JUNE

M	T	W	TH	F	S	S
				1	2	3
4	5	6	7	8	9	10
11	12	13	14	15	16	17
18	19	20	21	22	23	24
25	26	27	28	29	30	

June has _____ days

JULY

M	T	W	TH	F	S	S
						1
2	3	4	5	6	7	8
9	10	11	12	13	14	15
16	17	18	19	20	21	22
23	24	25	26	27	28	29
30	31					

July has _____ days

AUGUST

M	T	W	TH	F	S	S
	1	2	3	4	5	
6	7	8	9	10	11	12
13	14	15	16	17	18	19
20	21	22	23	24	25	26
27	28	29	30	31		

August has _____ days

SEPTEMBER

M	T	W	TH	F	S	S
					1	2
3	4	5	6	7	8	9
10	11	12	13	14	15	16
17	18	19	20	21	22	23
24	25	26	27	28	29	30

September has _____ days

OCTOBER

M	T	W	TH	F	S	S
1	2	3	4	5	6	7
8	9	10	11	12	13	14
15	16	17	18	19	20	21
22	23	24	25	26	27	28
29	30	31				

October has _____ days

NOVEMBER

M	T	W	TH	F	S	S
			1	2	3	4
5	6	7	8	9	10	11
12	13	14	15	16	17	18
19	20	21	22	23	24	25
26	27	28	29	30		

November has _____ days

DECEMBER

M	T	W	TH	F	S	S
					1	2
3	4	5	6	7	8	9
10	11	12	13	14	15	16
17	18	19	20	21	22	23
24	25	26	27	28	29	30
31						

December has _____ days

Circle your birthday in red.

Name _____

Spring and Summer

The year is divided into four seasons: Spring, Summer, Fall, and Winter.

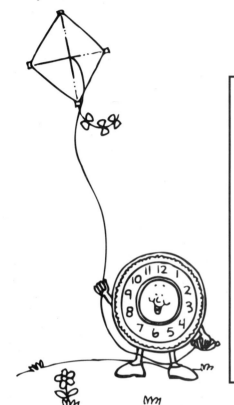

March, April, and May are spring months. What do you like to do best in spring? Draw or write your answer.

June, July, and August are summer months.
Draw a picture of your favorite summer activity.

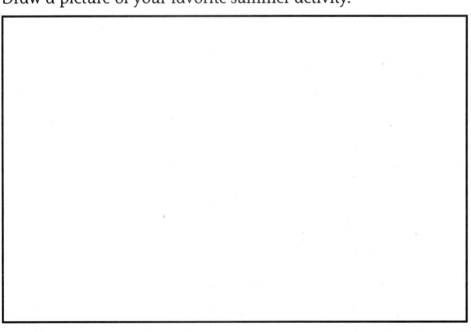

J209039

Name _____

Fall and Winter

September, October, and November are fall months. Do the leaves change colors where you live? How is fall different from spring?

_____
_____
_____
_____
_____
_____
_____
_____
_____

December, January, and February are winter months. In some parts of the country, winter can be very cold. What is a winter day like where you live?

_____
_____
_____
_____
_____
_____
_____
_____
_____

In Australia, December, January, and February are summer months.

Name _____

How Long Is a Year?

One year equals the time it takes for the Earth to make one complete revolution around the sun.

> The Earth travels about 66,000 miles per hour for a total of 580 million miles in one year.

A year is a long time:

31,536,000 seconds = 1 year
525,600 minutes = 1 year
8,760 hours = 1 year
365 days = 1 year
52 weeks = 1 year
12 months = 1 year

- A baby can be born, learn to crawl, and start to walk in one year.
- A year is how long you have to wait between one birthday and the next.
- It takes about one full year for a baby zebra to be born.

What are some other things that take a year?

_____

_____

Make a drawing that shows how much something can change in one year.

> Long, long, long ago, the Earth rotated faster than it does today. About 600 million years ago, one year would have contained 425 days. Since then, the rotation of the Earth has slowed. About 85 million years ago, there would have been about 370.3 days in a year.

J209039

Name _____

Leap Years

It takes the Earth 365 1/4 days to make one complete revolution around the sun. That means each year on Earth is 365 1/4 days long. What happens to the 1/4 day left over at the end of the year?

For three years in a row, we have 365 days. Every fourth year is called a *leap year*. We add one extra day to make up for the parts of days leftover for the last three years. That extra day is added at the end of February. Instead of 28 days, February has 29 days.

What would you do if you were born on February 29? Would you have to wait four years between birthdays?

A year is a leap year if the last two digits can be divided evenly by 4 with no remainder.

Are these leap years? Use the back of this page to work the division problems if you are not sure. Circle yes or no.

A.	1976	Yes	No
B.	1248	Yes	No
C.	1362	Yes	No
D.	1492	Yes	No
E.	2178	Yes	No
F.	1929	Yes	No
G.	1888	Yes	No
H.	2024	Yes	No
I.	1776	Yes	No
J.	1528	Yes	No
K.	1066	Yes	No
L.	1630	Yes	No
M.	2756	Yes	No

What year is this? _____ Is it a leap year? _____

When will the next leap year be? _____

What if at the end of each year we added one day that was only 6 hours long?

_____

_____

_____

_____

Name _____

Longer than a Year

We use special words to measure long periods of time.

| **10 years = 1 Decade** |

How many decades have your parents lived? _____

How old will you be in 10 years? _____

Draw or write about how you think your life will be different in 10 years.

| **100 years = 1 Century** |

What year was it 100 years ago? _____

Use reference books to find the answers to these questions.
Write your answers on another sheet of paper.

1. Who was president 100 years ago?

2. Did the telephone exist 100 years ago?

3. Name three people who were living 100 years ago.

4. List two things we have today that were not invented 100 years ago.

| **1,000 years = 1 Millennium** |

5. What year was it 1,000 years ago?

6. Why wasn't there a President of the United States that year?

| **1,000 times 1,000 = 1 million** |

The last of the dinosaurs died out more than 100 million years ago.

The slowest growing creature in the animal kingdom is a type of deep-sea clam that takes about 100 years to reach a length of 0.31 inches.

J209039

Let's Review

Fill in the blanks.

1. When the **minute hand** is on the 3, one-quarter of an hour (_____ minutes) has passed.

2. When the **minute hand** is on the 6, half of an hour (_____ minutes) has passed.

3. When the **minute hand** is on the 9, three-quarters of an hour (_____ minutes) have passed. It is now 15 minutes to the next hour.

Draw the correct hands to show the time.

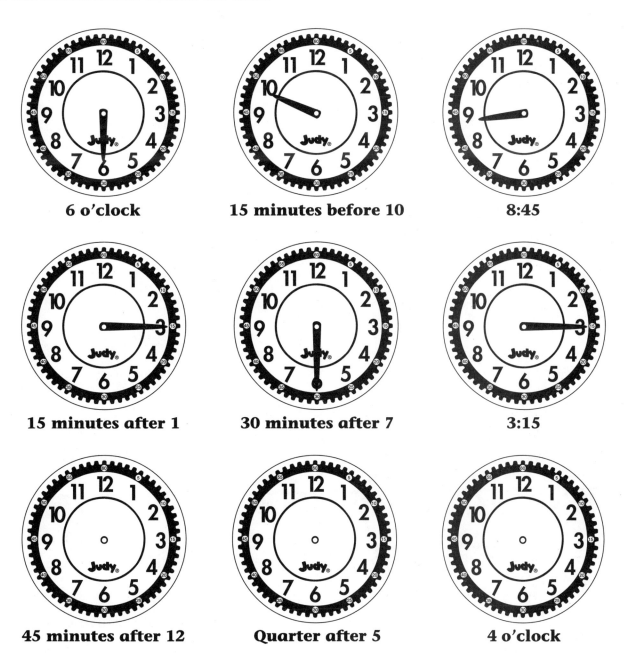

6 o'clock	**15 minutes before 10**	**8:45**
15 minutes after 1	**30 minutes after 7**	**3:15**
45 minutes after 12	**Quarter after 5**	**4 o'clock**

Match the Times

Connect the clocks with the correct time.

eleven minutes after ten

15 minutes after 7

11:45

4:33

1:19

12:45

15 minutes before 9

45 minutes after 6

quarter after 6

J209039

Name _____

Tick, Tock, Set the Clock

Draw the **minute hands** on these clocks to show the correct time.

3:22

12:02

6:28

11:07

9:14

2:47

10:51

7:58

5:21

8:36

J209039

Name _____

More or Less?

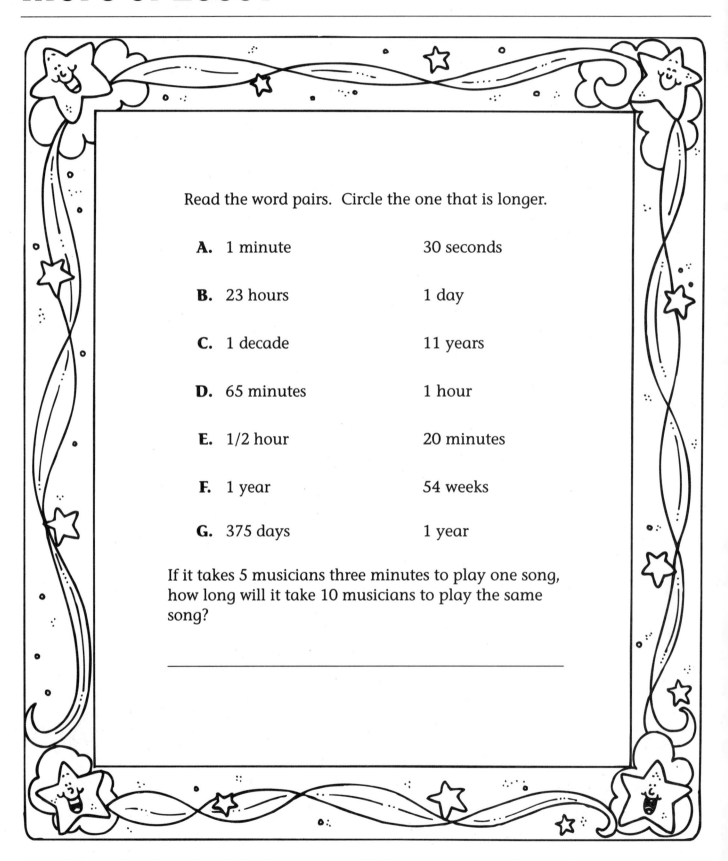

Read the word pairs. Circle the one that is longer.

A. 1 minute   30 seconds

B. 23 hours   1 day

C. 1 decade   11 years

D. 65 minutes   1 hour

E. 1/2 hour   20 minutes

F. 1 year   54 weeks

G. 375 days   1 year

If it takes 5 musicians three minutes to play one song, how long will it take 10 musicians to play the same song?

_____

                     J209039

Neat Books about Time

Allington, Dr. Richard L. and Kathleen Krull *Beginning to Learn about Time.* Raintree, 1983.

Anno, Mitasumasa. *Anno's Sundial.* Putnam, 1987.

Berry, Jow. *Every Kid's Guide to Using Time Wisely.* Childrens Press, 1987.

Breiter, Herta S. *Time and Clocks.* Raintree, 1978.

Burns, Marilyn. *This Book Is About Time.* Little, Brown, 1978.

Gibbons, Gail. *Clocks and How They Go.* Harper, 1979.

Gleiter, Jan. *Teddies Tell the Time.* Raintree, 1986.

Jennings, Terry. *Time.* Gloucester Press, 1988.

Perl, Lila. *Blue Monday and Friday the Thirteenth.* Ticknor, 1986.

Maestro, Betty. *Around the Clock with Harriet.* Crown, 1984.

Smoothey, Marion. *Let's Investigate Time, Distance and Speed.* Marshall Cavendish, 1993.

Ziner, Feenie and Elizabeth Thompson. *Time.* Childrens Press, 1982.

Zubrowski, Bernie. *Clocks: Building and Experimenting with Model Timepieces.* Boston Children's Museum, Morrow Junior Books, 1988.

Notes